Lordlings of Yore

The Game of Knights, Knaves and Necromancers

I0487395

ORIGINAL EDITION

Jon F. Baxley → Design
Trey C. Johnson → Original Program
Pat Boyette → Cover Art
Mike Neely → Illustrations

ENHANCED EDITION

Brian Wiser → Design, Layout, Editing
Bill Martens → Program Updates
Jon F. Baxley → Preface, Digital Assets

 Apple PugetSound Program Library Exchange

Lordlings of Yore

www.callapple.org

Paperback ISBN: 978-0-359-18785-0
Hardback ISBN: 978-0-359-18802-4

ACKNOWLEDGEMENTS

Lordlings of Yore was originally designed by Jon F. Baxley, programmed for the Apple II by Trey C. Johnson, and published by Softlore Corporation in 1983. The *Lordlings of Yore* original game and documentation published in 1983 are Copyright © 1983 Jon F. Baxley. All rights reserved.

We would like to thank Jon F. Baxley for his support, dedication, and contributions. This new manual and a limited edition box, produced in coordination with Jon F. Baxley and released with his permission, are copyright by A.P.P.L.E.. No claim to copyright over *Lordlings of Yore* is created outside of those portions created by A.P.P.L.E..

The modified Cover Art was originally created by Pat Boyette.
The Interior Illustrations were created by Mike Neely.
The new Cover, Manual, and Box were designed by Brian Wiser.

PRODUCTION

Brian Wiser → Art Remastering, Design, Layout, Editing
Bill Martens → Software Updates, Production
Jon F. Baxley → Scanning, Digital Conversion of Manual

DISCLAIMER

About Jon F. Baxley

Jon F. Baxley is an author, freelance writer, game designer and medieval historian from San Antonio, Texas. His latest major work is a three book fantasy series entitled *The Scythian Stone Saga* set in Scotland in the late 900s. The series is available in print and eBook formats from Amazon and other fine retailers.

A 1969 University of Texas at Arlington graduate, Jon served with the U.S. Army, worked as a golf professional, and consulted for the United States Information Agency in the former Soviet Union. Having been a full-time writer and author for many years, Jon eventually turned his attention to fiction writing and has never looked back.

When someone asks about his writing experiences, Jon answers with, "Ask not what a publisher can do for you. Ask what you can do for your publisher." The author's email address is: FiveStarAuthor@aol.com.

About the Producers

Brian Wiser

Brian Wiser is a long-time consultant, enthusiast and historian of Apple, the Apple II and Macintosh. Steve Wozniak and Steve Jobs, as well as *Creative Computing, Nibble, InCider,* and *A+* magazines were early influences.

Brian designed, edited, and co-produced many books including: *Nibble Viewpoints: Business Insights From The Computing Revolution, Cyber Jack: The Adventures of Robert Clardy and Synergistic Software, Synergistic Software: The Early Games, The Colossal Computer Cartoon Book: Enhanced Edition, What's Where in the Apple: Enhanced Edition,* and *The WOZPAK: Special Edition* – an important Apple II historical book with Steve Wozniak's restored original, technical handwritten notes.

He passionately preserves and archives all facets of Apple's history, and noteworthy related companies such as Beagle Bros and Applied Engineering, featured on AppleArchives.com. His writing, interviews and books are featured on the technology news site CallApple.org and in *Call-A.P.P.L.E.* magazine that he co-produces. Brian also co-produced the retro iOS game *Structris.*

In 2005, Brian was cast as an extra in Joss Whedon's movie *Serenity*, leading him to being a producer and director for the documentary film *Done The Impossible: The Fans' Tale of Firefly & Serenity.* He brought some of the *Firefly* cast aboard his Browncoat Cruise and recruited several of the *Firefly* cast to appear in a film for charity. Brian speaks about his adventures to large audiences at conventions around the country.

Bill Martens

Bill Martens is a systems engineer specializing in office infrastructures and has been programming since 1976. The DEC PDP 11/40 with ASR-33 Teletypes and CRT's were his first computing platforms with his first forays in the Apple world coming with the Apple II computer.

Influences in Bill's computing life came from *Byte* magazine, *Creative Computing* magazine, and *Call-A.P.P.L.E.* magazine as well as his mentors Samuel Perkins, Don Williams, Joff Morgan, and Mike Christensen.

Bill is a co-producer of many books including *What's Where in the Apple: Enhanced Edition*, *The WOZPAK: Special Edition*, *Nibble Viewpoints: Business Insights From The Computing Revolution*, and co-programmer for the iOS version of the retro game *Structris*. He has written many articles which have appeared in user group newsletters and magazines such as *Call-A.P.P.L.E.*.

Bill worked for Apple Pugetsound Program Library Exchange (A.P.P.L.E.) under Val Golding and Dick Hubert as a data manager and programmer in the 1980s, and is the current president of the A.P.P.L.E. user group established in 1978. He reorganized A.P.P.L.E. and restarted *Call-A.P.P.L.E.* magazine in 2002. He is the production editor for the A.P.P.L.E. website CallApple.org, writes science fiction novels in his spare time, and is a retired semi-pro football player.

Lordlings of Yore

Contents

Hints of Play

Notes for Programming Wizards

Your Adventure Awaits...

Preface

I'm Jon Baxley, the original designer of *Lordlings of Yore*. If you're reading this, I will make a leap of faith and assume that you are among the legions of inveterate Apple computer users who are excited by the opportunity to relive some of the very earliest days of computing bliss when 48K games were state of the art.

Notice I said 48K – not 48 megabytes – which is probably far less than the computing power of your wristwatch. Nostalgia games are all the rage again, provided you can find an original working copy of the games players cherished for decades and that's not always easy.

Thanks to the Apple Pugetsound Program Library Exchange (A.P.P.L.E.) you can now find a cross-selection of some of the hottest Apple titles of the 1980s and 1990s that will sweep you back to the genesis of the computer gaming industry. And I know something about that era, having met Steve Jobs in my Apple dealership at a time when only he and a few others had the vision to see where the home computing industry was headed. Ah, if only I had kept my Apple stock.

I'm pleased and humbled to be a small part of this resurrection effort. I hope you will enjoy the process of rediscovering games you and your friends thought lost forever. Now, don your chainmail, pop that game disk in your old Apple and "cry havoc." *Lordlings of Yore* is back!

Jon F. Baxley

September 2018

The Evolution of "Lordlings of Yore" and Why That Might Matter to You

by Jon F. Baxley

In the very early days of Apple when home computers were as scarce as jumbo jets, the market for anything fun to play on the Apple II and IIe lay wide open. Very few multiplayer games existed and for hardcore gamers like myself, any game worth its salt *had* to have viable and worthy computer opponents who could actually win a game against humans. Chess games were okay as were checkers and a few other one-on-one products but none of those gave you the anxiety and edge-of-your-seat uncertainty of what was about to happen in the game.

At that time (the early 1980s) I happened to be in the enviable position of a total novice when it came to home computers. That is, until I was hired to manage one of the very first Apple Computer dealerships located inside a major mall. Believe it or not, the name of the store was *Expensive Toys For Big Boys* and within a very short time, we became *the* place to buy Apple Computers in our area. The Apple II Plus had just come out when we got a visit from a slight young man named Steve Jobs, who I had never heard of. He gave us the lowdown on the Apple IIe and his future blockbuster product, the Macintosh.

My question to him was, "What about software? What are people supposed to *do* with their Apple once they get it home?" Mr. Jobs gave us a wry answer of, "Anything they want," and that stuck with me for the next eight years.

Coming from a board game publishing background, I quickly seized on the need for games as well as work programs like *VisiCalc*, a spreadsheet dynamo that could do things we never dreamed of at that early stage of the business. It became one of our best selling items and helped us market hundreds of Apples to folks who had never seen a home computer.

Many months later and with hundreds of Apples sold, I began to conceive of a game system that would encompass all of the things I had wished for when designing board games for the 'wargaming' market – foremost of which was to have someone to battle against who was always available for a game. I met a young man, Trey C. Johnson, who had spent months teaching himself to program on the Apple and together we embarked on the trial and error process of making computer players smart enough to be worth the cost of a game package. A year later, having designed, re-designed, tested and tested again for what seemed like a million hours, the first working copy of *Lordlings of Yore* was born.

Why Apple II, you might ask – as other platforms had come online by the mid-1980s? No other home computer offered the promise of mass market game appeal the way the new Apples did, despite the relatively poor sales numbers for both the Lisa and the Macintosh. Color in the game was extremely important as was speed, ease of use, and upgrade prospects for systems that by now had progressed all the way up to a 'whopping' 128K. And, even though Tandy and IBM both expressed an interest in *Lordlings of Yore* for their PC's, they simply did not see far enough ahead to realize that computer gaming was destined to become one of the most powerful driving forces in home computer evolution. Steve Jobs used the phrase, "Users from 8 to 80," often and he couldn't have been more correct.

What makes Lordlings of Yore special? Longevity is always a hallmark for quality products and here we are some thirty years later offering gamers a chance to enjoy this design that has never been duplicated. Over the years I have heard from gamers complaining that the computer players (cp's) are too difficult to beat. My answer has always been, "Would you rather learn chess from Kasparov or a 10-year-old down at the YMCA?" For its era and its minimal memory space, the LOY game system is unsurpassed. Yes, the cp's will tend to gang up on you but I promise you they will make you a better player. Then when you match wits with three of your friends in an all-human game, you will know everything you need to know to win. Not many games give you that kind of satisfaction. Now, put this rule booklet aside and get on with the blood-letting. The title "Lord of the Realm" awaits!

Lordlings of Yore

Equipment Required

An Apple II Plus, IIe, IIc, IIGS, or emulator with at least 48K RAM, one disk drive, and monitor are required. A printer is optional and may enhance your gaming experience. No joystick or other external devices are required to play this game. A disk image of *Lordlings of Yore* can be freely downloaded from the publisher's site: www.callapple.org. A limited edition box and physical disk are also available for purchase.

It is suggested that players have a pencil and paper upon which to make notes and draw maps as the game progresses. If you do not have a printer, you are allowed to reproduce the map facsimile provided with this game. All other materials are copyrighted and cannot be reproduced for any reason.

General Description

Lordlings of Yore is a game of strategy, tactics and diplomacy set in the era of knights and chivalry. You and your opponents begin the game with an equal number of troops and wealth (unless a handicap is used for play balance), but with a different geographical situation in your respective SHIRE (an English county).

The object is for you to eliminate the opposing lordlings (minor lords or castle holders) and ultimately become the Lord of the Realm. You control your shire in a manner similar to that of a feudal lord with taxation from peasants being your primary means of support. Your army represents your main element of control in the game.

1

Lordlings of Yore can be played by one person matching wits with three computer opponents, two people against two computer players, three humans against one "cp" or the best of all worlds, four humans vying for victory against each other. Levels of difficulty can be altered to enhance game play or for introducing new players to the game. In addition, players are able to add more terrain features to the map for extended variability.

This game system combines many of the elements of a fantasy game and a strategy game, as well as those of an adventure game. We have chosen to call this type of computer game a "fantegy" and no doubt you will soon see why. The game mechanics are quite simple but that is where the simplicity ends.

Much of a player's actions are made with no knowledge of what opponents are doing or have done. Just imagine a chess game played where you can only see your half of the board. Combat is resolved by the most efficient, realistic and historically accurate system available in 48K. Each move brings a new situation to light and the inability to see what opponents are doing makes for an exciting and interesting strategy game.

A Brief History of the Period

The dark times of medieval history were fraught with war, civil war and unrest in the countryside. Brothers battled brothers, fathers fought sons and everywhere blood was spilled on the field of honor – all in the vain attempt to establish "rightful ownership" of titles and properties not yet clearly owned by anyone.

The ancient rules of chivalry still regulated warfare to some extent but gone were the days of single combat between knights of opposing armies. In the lordlings era, huge masses of heavily armored and mounted warriors would clash in day long battles to decide an issue in question. Hundreds of foot soldiers or men-at-arms were recruited from the local area to join in these intense, bloody engagements knowing all the while that their own farms and villages were likely to be the prize for the victors. Battles sometimes raged into the night and the following day until one army or the other emerged bloodied but victorious. Casualties could be horrendous as were the terrible effects of burned hovels and ruined farms on both sides of the conflict.

More often than not, this whole process would be repeated again and again by succeeding waves of intruders all bent on the same path of domination. Such was the pattern of establishing "order" in these difficult times. Clearly defined objectives rarely existed and few of the local inhabitants had much to say about how they were to be treated. Their lands were frequently forfeited to the ruler of the day. What pittance of gold or silver they accrued usually went for taxes, their crops and livestock taken in lieu of cash. All this was done "in the name of the king" – whoever *that* was – for rarely did peasants know or care who currently governed their tiny corner of the world.

Peasants suffered even more under a new and harsher system of control called "feudalism" fostered on the European continent and adopted across much of the rest of the land. Peasants became "chattel"

for any army moving through their area, never knowing when the next new ruler's flags would appear on the horizon. Sometimes this would have a positive outcome for the local villages as the new lordling would establish their version of law and order where there had been none before. Or, a cruel tyrant who had ruled by fear and intimation would be eliminated, leaving a power vacuum in the shire. Going from feast to famine became all too familiar for most peasants as a result.

Eventually feudalism gave way to a more equitable system for the masses. Property ownership became more established as did the laws that governed the land. This meant peasant land owners could begin to reap the benefits of their own labor instead of always working to fill the king's coffers. You will find that the power of appeasement in Lordlings of Yore will pay benefits for you and your peasants. Don't ignore it or you are destined to repeat the failures of feudalism.

BEGINNING PLAY

Players begin by selecting a new or old game, any terrain modifiers and the number of humans playing. You then enter a secret password and the name you intend for your shire to be called. Names can be up to ten characters while passwords are limited to four characters so as not to be forgotten (even from game to game as LOY can be saved in progress). Should you forget your password, a new one can be assigned by *saving*

```
----====###*###====----

PICK YOUR TERRAIN MODIFIERS, M'LORD:

    <1> MORE MOUNTAINS
    <2> MORE FORESTS
    <3> MORE SWAMPS
    <4> MORE MOUNTAINS & FORESTS
    <5> MORE MOUNTAINS & SWAMPS
    <6> MORE FORESTS & SWAMPS
    <7> MORE OF EVERYTHING
    <8> NO MODIFICATIONS

    ----====###*###====----
```

the game and re-entering new ones for each player. If you attempt to enter an incorrect password three times, *you will lose your turn* so don't forget it! Lastly, players will choose a handicap level between one (Normal Treasury/Garrison) and four (Larger Treasury/Garrison).

Once all players have signed in, there is a short delay while the maps are "fetched" by your squires. Each time you begin a new game the maps are redrawn so that no two games will ever be alike. The order of play is then randomly determined and you are assigned a player number. Computer players (cp's) are never assigned as Player 1. Player 1 always begins the game in the upper left portion of the board, Player 2 starts in the upper right portion, Player 3 in the lower left portion and Player 4 in the lower right.

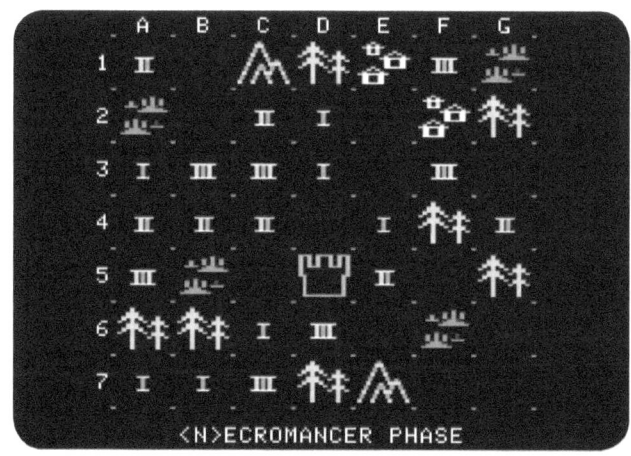

A turn or day indicator is provided which helps players keep track of turns. From this point on, players move and perform actions independently. Ideally, human players should not be allowed to observe other human moves and actions. This will not be necessary when computer players are moving as nothing shows on the monitor except a minute glass that indicates how much of a cp's turn is left.

After entering your password at the beginning of a turn, you will be shown your SHIRE ESTEEM, the amount of taxes collected that day, any messages and then the map of your shire. Various terrain features will be indicated, and any storms present and the flags of friendly and enemy units will be displayed.

Flags represent units consisting of knights and men-at-arms. Only such terrain and enemy flags as are IN SIGHT of your flags will be placed on the map when you are in enemy shires. *In sight* is defined as the eight squares (or hectares) immediately surrounding a flag. Shire borders cannot be seen across, therefore you will not be able to see anything in an enemy shire until you have actually crossed over into that shire.

STRATEGY

Terrain is probably the most important element in determining strategy in this game. If you are attempting to battle three cp's, select *more* terrain at the beginning of the game setup. Consider such things as how far your castle is from a hostile border or where most of your population is centered. Mountains are important as they restrict movement. When battling human opponents, players should also consider personalities. Aggressive players will often make big moves early. Less aggressive ones are more likely to wait for others to force the issues.

Analyze which areas of your shire are the most vulnerable to attack and decide if that is where you need to deploy troops first. Always remember that early on in LOY, you have no way of knowing what other players are doing and that you cannot cover *all* of your objectives in the first few "days" in the game. Just like in medieval times, protection and control of your peasants and their villages is especially important because without peasants to tax, lordlings cannot field an army and without an army, you may as well accidentally hit the reset button.

PEASANTS

Players begin the game with 5,000 peasants under their control in their home shire. Each Roman numeral on the map represents 100 peasants and each village represents 400 peasants. Every peasant you control contributes one gold piece to your treasury every turn. Control of these peasants is always determined at the beginning of your turn and is considered automatic in your home shire provided no enemy units (flags) have moved onto any of your peasant squares or villages.

If any of your peasants are under the control of an enemy's troops, you must defeat the enemy unit and force it off of that peasant hectare to regain control of those peasants. To control peasants in any shire other than your own, you MUST have a unit located *in the square at the beginning of your turn*. It is not sufficient to have simply passed through a square to receive the taxation from it.

Think of it this way. Would a medieval peasant come running after a tax collector and his troops to pay taxes once they had left the area? Probably not – thus it is the same in *Lordlings of Yore*.

Game Phases

Each turn or day in *Lordlings of Yore* is divided into 6 PHASES:

1. [N]ecromancer
2. [T]reasury
3. [D]eployment
4. [M]ovement
5. Combat
6. Options

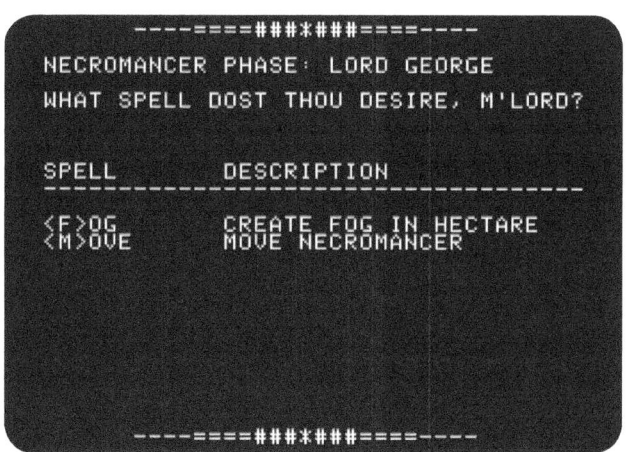

The first phase of a turn is the "**[N]ecromancer**" phase in which you are allowed to cast *one* spell for that turn. This spell must be chosen from the spells listed on the Necromancer menu. If you did not purchase a spell in a previous [T]reasury phase, you will be limited to casting one of the 'free' spells a Necromancer always has at hand.

Once you have cast your spell, the phase ends and moves on to the [T]reasury phase. If you do not wish to employ your Necromancer in a given turn, simply press [Return] to proceed to the next phase.

```
----====########====----
TREASURY PHASE FOR: LORD GEORGE
TREASURY BALANCE:  20000 GOLD PIECES
     ITEMS                COST
-----------------------------------
  <K>NIGHTS          1000 GOLD PCS.
  <M>EN-AT-ARMS       100 GOLD PCS.
  <S>PELLS          (SEE SPELLS)
  <A>PPEASEMENT      1000 GOLD PCS.
  <B>RIBERY          ???? GOLD PCS.
  <I>NTELLIGENCE      50? GOLD PCS.
   (M'LORD MAY SPEND UP TO 30000)
----====########====----
```

The second phase of a turn is the "**[T]reasury**" phase. During this phase you will allocate or spend the accumulated treasury money you have gained through taxation of your peasants. Gold can be spent on:

[K]nights   Your main fighting elements.

[M]en-at-Arms Garrison troops and foot soldiers that fight in a one to ten ration to knights.

[S]pells   For the necromancer (only one at a time can be accumulated besides the free spells).

[A]ppeasement Gold spent to keep the peasants happy and to prevent uprisings or other troubles in your shire.

[B]ribery   Can be an attempt to gain cooperation from another player for whatever reason.

[I]ntelligence Information bribed from the local "knaves" to help you determine (for example) how large an enemy unit is before you attack it.

When you have finished all of your spending, press [Return] to go on to the next phase. If you have spent all of your gold or (gasp) reached a negative balance, the [T]reasury phase will end automatically. If you begin your turn with a zero or negative balance, the [T]reasury phase will be skipped entirely. Try not to let that happen – especially against other human players!

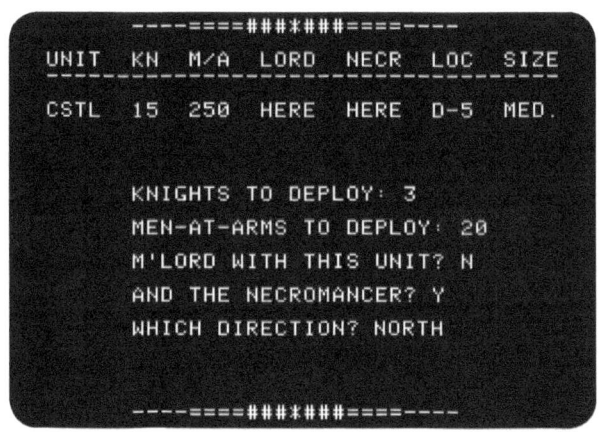

```
    ----====########====----
  UNIT  KN  M/A  LORD  NECR  LOC  SIZE
  ------------------------------------
  CSTL  15  250  HERE  HERE  D-5  MED.


    KNIGHTS TO DEPLOY: 3
    MEN-AT-ARMS TO DEPLOY: 20
    M'LORD WITH THIS UNIT? N
    AND THE NECROMANCER? Y
    WHICH DIRECTION? NORTH


    ----====########====----
```

The third phase of a turn is the "**[D]eployment**" phase. This is when you will form units from the troops in your castle garrison. As a flag is deployed, you must assign a number of knights or men-at-arms (or both) to the unit as well as a lordling or necromancer if you so desire. You will give that unit a [N]orth, [S]outh, [E]ast, or [W]est direction to march.

A deployed unit is assigned your player number and you then give each one a letter designation for its flag. That letter is important as it can help players remember which unit has which soldiers, etc. For example, should you desire to deploy a lordling with a unit, you could secretly designate it 1-X where only you will know that X has a lordling in the battle array. Or you can simply deploy your units in alphabetical order and keep track of them on paper.

Some players devise their own "code" for letter designations that instantly tells them what troops are in a particular unit. For example, 1-D might mean that there are only four men-at-arms in that unit (D being the fourth letter of the alphabet). The possibilities are endless.

When you have no more troops to deploy, the phase ends or you can press [Return] to move on in the game. If you have no troops available for deployment or already have the maximum of 26 units deployed at the end of the [T]reasury phase, the [D]eployment phase will be skipped.

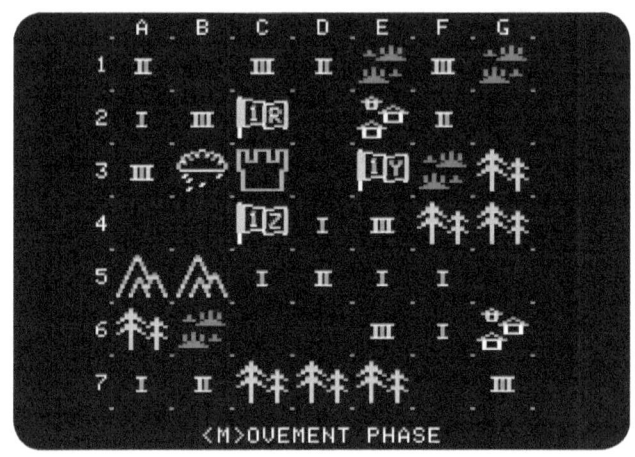

<M>OVEMENT PHASE

The fourth phase of a turn is "**[M]ovement**." In this phase, you may move units deployed from previous turns. Units deployed in the current turn have already moved and thus are not able to move again. Each unit is moved by using [N]orth, [S]outh, [E]ast or [W]est on the keyboard until all units are moved. North on the game board is always to the top of the screen, south to the bottom, east is to the right and west is to the left. Once all units have been moved, the phase will end and go directly to the Combat phase or if there are no battles to resolve, on to Options. As always, you may end a phase any time by pressing the [Return] key.

The fifth phase of a turn is "**Combat**." All battles caused by your [M]ovement phase are now resolved one at a time *in the order your movement determined*. This can be very important in the flow of the game so make sure you understand this concept. The first unit you moved into contact with an enemy unit will *always* be the first battle resolved. You will observe each battle as it is being fought on the Battle Array screen. Any *advances* or *retreats* will be performed by the computer after each individual battle before the next battle is resolved. You have no control over these movements so be sure you refer to *Movement After Combat* later in these rules as this element in the game can be absolutely critical to your success.

IMPORTANT NOTE: Movement After Combat *can* cause a domino effect by forcing a retreating or advancing unit to blunder into another enemy unit, resulting in *another* battle that will be resolved *after* all other initial battles have been fought. Just think of this as beaten soldiers running away from one fight, only to find themselves blindly rushing into another fight and so on. Or, victorious knights unable to stop their charge and advancing straight into more enemy troops. This can happen often in LOY and it was not uncommon at all on medieval battlefields. Bottom line: combat resolution will *never leave two units in the same hectare* at the end of a turn. Whole units can be destroyed as a result, so be sure you read the section on combat thoroughly.

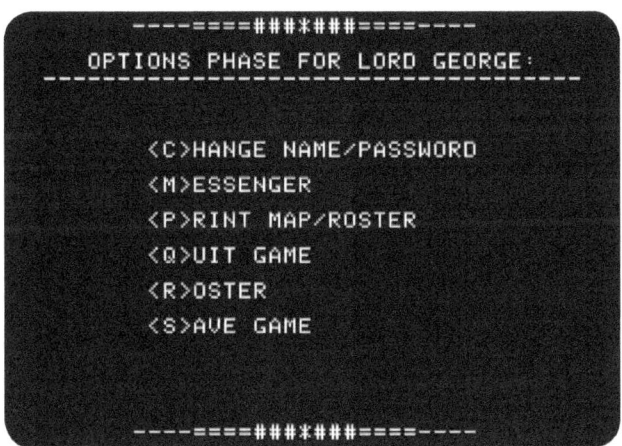

```
------=====########======-----
   OPTIONS PHASE FOR LORD GEORGE:
------------------------------------

     <C>HANGE NAME/PASSWORD
     <M>ESSENGER
     <P>RINT MAP/ROSTER
     <Q>UIT GAME
     <R>OSTER
     <S>AVE GAME



------=====########======-----
```

The sixth and last phase of a turn is the "**Options**" phase. Players are first shown any special events that have or will occur as well as the effects of those events if appropriate (see "Appeasement" on page 27). You will then have the opportunity to [C]hange your shire name or password, send a [M]essage to another player, [P]rint a map of your shire or roster (requires a printer), [Q]uit the game, look at your [R]oster or [S]ave the game in progress for future play. You can end your turn by pressing [Return] when you have finished all activities in the sixth phase.

To speed up game play, players can skip the first four phases as they appear on the monitor by pressing [Return]. *Caution:* once a phase is skipped, you will *not* be able to go back to it. Combat will always be resolved before the next player's turn begins and the Options phase is automatic at the end of every turn. Each turn goes through all six phases unless the computer determines that a phase is unavailable.

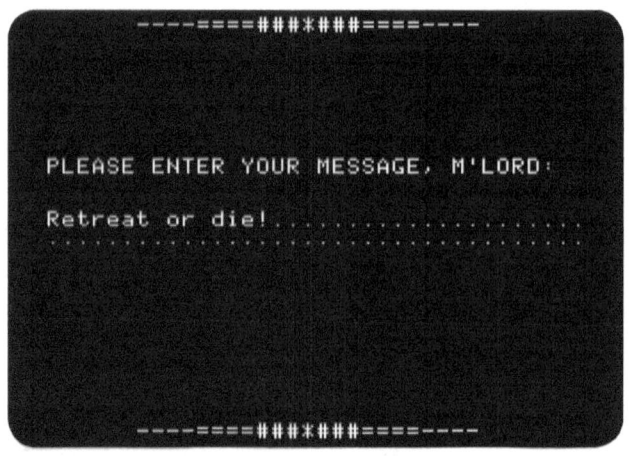

```
        ----====###*###====----



   PLEASE ENTER YOUR MESSAGE, M'LORD:

   Retreat or die!.......................
   .......................................



        ----====###*###====----
```

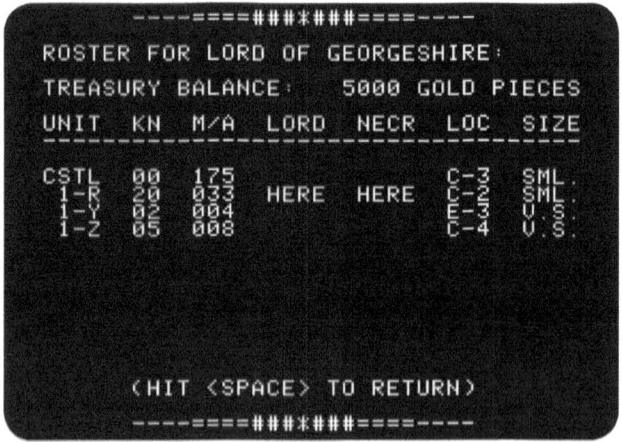

```
        ----====###*###====----
   ROSTER FOR LORD OF GEORGESHIRE:
   TREASURY BALANCE:    5000 GOLD PIECES
   UNIT  KN  M/A  LORD   NECR   LOC   SIZE
   ----------------------------------------
   CSTL  00  175                     C-3   SML.
   1-R   20  033  HERE   HERE        C-2   SML.
   1-Y   02  004                     E-3   V.S.
   1-Z   05  008                     C-4   V.S.




          (HIT <SPACE> TO RETURN)
        ----====###*###====----
```

The [R]oster option may be used during any phase except [N]ecromancer so that players can review their troops, determine strengths, locations and status. It is highly advisable to do so before entering the [N]ecromancer phase as combat with enemy units can cause unforeseen changes in a player's situation as can spells cast by your enemies since your last turn.

[N]ecromancer Phase

The following list of spells available to your necromancer (or wizard, if you prefer) outlines the type of spell, the cost and the effect that spell *should* create. Notice that the effect may not necessarily be what you expect, as spells have a nasty way of not turning out correctly or causing an unforeseen result.

Lordlings do not automatically get all of these spells at the outset of the game. You must use gold to compensate your wizard for bringing his great talents to bear on your behalf.

Necromancers can cast only one spell per turn and *only* during the [N]ecromancer phase. Spells last the duration of turns indicated unless [E]liminated earlier or your wizard is killed or you [Q]uit the game.

Spells must be cast without the benefit of seeing the shire maps so be very careful to think ahead to when and *where* the spell may unfold.

Some spells cost nothing as they are skills any necromancer worth his salt would be able to perform. Some spells are quite expensive, but then, the results may be well worth the cost.

Learn these spells well – practice them to see the effects. As your game skills improve, spell casting may be the one ability that gives you an edge over other players, particularly the cp's.

The Spells

[A]dvance   Advance one unit one extra hectare anywhere in the shires this turn. The unit chosen may be any unit of your army and it may be advanced to any vacant adjacent square that unit could normally move into. In other words, no movement into friendly or enemy occupied squares or any movement that under normal circumstances would be illegal. An illegal move *may* cause a unit to be destroyed so use this spell carefully. **Cost = 2,000 gold pieces**

[B]last   Destroy (eliminate) any unit anywhere in the four shires except a unit in the same square with a lordling, necromancer or castle. You should pick a target during the previous turn (or one you can actually see on the map) and hope it is still available (not moved into a castle, already eliminated, etc.) This spell has no effect on a dragon. **Cost = 5,000 gold pieces**

[C]reate   Create a maelstrom (violent storm) in any hectare anywhere in the four shires except those containing a castle, fog, dragon or maelstrom. The storm lasts two turns and prohibits any movement or combat into or out of that hectare for those two turns. Only one maelstrom can be created by each player at any given time. **Cost = 3,000 gold pieces**

[D]ragon   Conjure a dragon in any *vacant* square. The chosen hectare cannot contain terrain features, population, flags or the results of other spells. Dragons remain on the board from three to seven turns and *may* move randomly each turn. Units may never move into or through a dragon square without fighting it. Dragons can be destroyed by combat or by spells. Only one dragon can be created by a player at a time. **Cost = 10,000 gold pieces**

[E]liminate   Eliminate a mountain from the map or destroy an existing dragon. You must specify which to eliminate and enter its location on the shire map. **Cost = 15,000 gold pieces**

[F]og	Create a fog in any hectare except where a castle, dragon or maelstrom is already located. Fog lasts for one turn and reduces the combat ability of any defending unit in that square by one-half. For example, a unit consisting of six knights would be calculated for combat as only three knights. A unit of four men-at-arms would defend as two only. **Cost = FREE**
[M]ove	Move the necromancer from one of your units or your castle directly to another unit anywhere in the shires. Normal movement can then be performed with that unit *in that turn*. You must specify the exact coordinate for the necromancer to move to when casting this spell. **Cost = FREE**
[S]ight	"See" what an enemy unit consists of. The necromancer will be told how many knights, men-at-arms, wizards or lordlings are with the unit. You must specify exactly which unit by number and letter you wish to have the wizard identify. **Cost = 1,000 gold pieces**
[T]ransport	Transport up to ten knights (not men-at-arms) from your castle to any one of your units anywhere in the shires. You must specify the unit you wish to transport to and that unit must be able to take the number of knights you are sending without going over the 99 knights per unit limit. Troops transported may move normally and fight *in the same turn transported*. If your lordling is in the castle from which you are transporting troops, you may opt to send him with the knights. **Cost = 7,500 gold pieces**
[X]tricate Spell	Transport your lordling from anywhere in the shires back to your home castle. This is a very useful spell but be careful *when you use it*. **Cost = Your entire treasury on hand (minimum 5,000 gold pieces.)**

[T]REASURY PHASE

Your treasury is always maintained in your castle and is increased from turn to turn by taxation of peasants. Taxation is determined by the number of peasants you control at the beginning of a turn (see "Peasants" on page 7). Gold spent during the [T]reasury phase is subtracted from your treasury balance and the current amount available is always shown on the treasury menu and the troop roster.

You may spend your gold on any of the items listed on the menu or save it from turn to turn in order to afford more expensive items. Treasury gold can be affected by random events throughout the game (see "Appeasement" on page 27).

Generally, the higher you keep your shire esteem (how much the peasants like you), the more likely you are to see an increase in your treasury but sadly this is not always the case. Listed below are the items you can spend your gold on and the purpose of those items.

Treasury Items

ITEM	COST	PURPOSE
[K]nights	1,000 Gold Pieces Each	Mounted Warriors
[M]en-at-arms	100 Gold Pieces Each	Foot Soldiers
[A]dvance Spell	2,000 Gold Pieces Each	(See Necromancer Spells)
[B]last Spell	5,000 Gold Pieces Each	(See Necromancer Spells)
[C]reate Spell	3,000 Gold Pieces Each	(See Necromancer Spells)
[D]ragon Spell	10,000 Gold Pieces Each	(See Necromancer Spells)
[E]liminate Spell	15,000 Gold Pieces Each	(See Necromancer Spells)
[F]og Spell	This is a FREE spell!	(See Necromancer Spells)
[M]ove Spell	A FREE spell!	(See Necromancer Spells)
[S]light Spell	1,000 Gold Pieces Each	(See Necromancer Spells)
[T]ransport Spell	7,500 Gold Pieces Each	(See Necromancer Spells)
[X]tricate Spell	Your Entire Treasury (5,000 gold pieces minimum)	(See Necromancer Spells)

Other Items

ITEM	COST	PURPOSE
[A]ppeasement	1,000 Gold Pieces Each	Used to Influence Events
[B]ribery	Player's Discretion	Used to Influence Others
[I]ntelligence	Negotiable Amounts	Used to Influence Knaves

Players may spend up to *one and a half times* their actual treasury balance on any given turn with any deficit amounts to be made up from taxation on the *next* turn. That's right – like any big government, lordlings can spend more than they have on hand with the hope that any shortfalls will be made up another day. *Be careful with this option.* Reckless deficit spending can lead to subsequent problems that can domino in this game a lot faster than you might think. NOTE: You must have a positive balance before being allowed to buy *anything* during a [T]reasury phase. If you have a negative balance at the start of your turn, the [T]reasury phase will be skipped, leaving you wondering what happened to that phase, so stay aware of your gold balance at all times.

[D]EPLOYMENT PHASE

During this phase, players may deploy units in whatever order they decide as long as (1) no more than 26 of a player's units are on the board at one time; (2) no more than 99 knights or 999 men-at-arms are deployed in a single unit; and (3) there is sufficient room in the adjoining castle squares to physically deploy the units without violating (2) above. All troops purchased during the [T]reasury phase are initially assigned to your castle garrison.

In addition, castles have an intrinsic strength of 100 men-at-arms which will be replaced automatically by purchased troops if reduced during a previous combat phase. Your castle can never exceed the 99/999 limit so be sure you keep track of all newly acquired forces.

As you are deploying your units, you will be asked if m'lord will join the unit just created. If you wish to move and fight with that unit, simply answer [Y]es. You may at any time join another unit that moves into the hectare you occupy but a lordling is never allowed to travel alone unless forced to by an [X]tricate spell.

Should the unit a lordling travels with be advanced, retreated or <gasp> eliminated, the lordling suffers the same fate. This is the biggest risk to committing yourself in combat. The advantage is, your presence with a unit has a positive effect on that unit's fighting ability. You should always keep your lordling with as big a unit as possible when away from your castle to avoid any nasty surprises. Some of the same risks and benefits apply when a necromancer is travelling with a unit. Refer to the "Terrain Effects" table on page 24 for clarification on this.

Once you have assigned a unit its knights and men-at-arms, a lordling or a necromancer, you will then be asked for a direction to deploy from the castle. This will always be [N], [S], [E] or [W] as in movement and is subject to the restrictions mentioned above. After you assign a unit its ID letter, that flag will flash on the monitor and move in its ordered direction. Repeat this procedure for every unit you deploy.

[M]OVEMENT PHASE

Movement in *Lordlings of Yore* is done by tapping the [N]orth, [S]outh, [E]ast or [W]est keys on the keyboard for each unit previously deployed. Each unit deployed in a previous turn can move ONE hectare during this phase but only once per turn. Newly deployed units have already moved during deployment and thus cannot move again. Unlike chess, players cannot move a unit, change their mind and attempt to move it back or in another direction.

You may split a unit into several new units by using [D]eploy during movement, which is similar to deploying from a castle. You may also combine units at this time by moving them into a common square under one flag. Once you have moved a unit, it cannot be moved or deployed again except as a result of combat. Also – if you deploy part of one unit onto a second unit that has not yet moved, you will prohibit that second unit from moving this turn.

A unit's flag will flash on the screen to prompt you to move it in sequence. This sequence is always from A to Z, regardless of what letters you have assigned to your units or in what order. If you do not wish to move a unit, press [H]old and the unit's movement will be ended. Should you need to bypass one unit temporarily, tap the [Space Bar] and go on to the next unit. Once you have gone through a complete cycle with all units, you will be allowed to go back and pick up any 'stragglers' that were initially bypassed. Repeat the process until all units have been ordered to hold or move.

Units that are in other shires will be moved in the same manner until you have completed movement for all of your troops or until you tap [Return]. You may avoid going through each unit in a shire individually if you wish by pressing [P]ass to go onto the next shire. You will be allowed to come back to any shire passed. You can also terminate movement in any shire without ending your [M]ovement phase by pressing [Esc]. This will end movement in that shire and avoid the necessity of going through every unit when you have none that you wish to move.

Once you have finished all movement, press the [Return] and the movement phase will end. This brings on the combat phase or options phase if no combat is needed. Players should make notes of where units are, etc. to help in their next turn.

Limited Intelligence

In order to further enhance the "fog of war" aspect in *Lordlings of Yore*, players are not allowed to see what is on the other shire maps except that which is **in sight** of your units. As you move into enemy shires, mapping of the terrain becomes more complete. In the process of moving, you will also encounter enemy flags.

You may choose to identify some of these units ahead of time by using a [S]ight spell during the necromancer phase or by paying for *Limited Intelligence* from local knaves who will barter their information to you during your treasury phase. A knave will only tell you if an enemy force is:

→ Very Small (less than 11 knights or the equivalent in men-at-arms)

→ Small (11 to 25)

→ Medium (26 to 50)

→ Large (51 to 75)

→ Huge (76 to 99)

This information is not always totally accurate so don't bet the castle on it. You must barter for intelligence during the treasury phase for as many units as you can afford or feel the need to discover. You may only get information on units that are in sight of your troops. You must have units deployed in order to barter for intelligence on any enemy units.

NOTE: Maps of enemy shires will only show enemy units that are *still in sight of your units* no matter how many times you have moved into or through those shires.

There is no limit (other than your gold balance) on how much you can spend for intelligence. Keep in mind that offering too little gold to knaves can cause them to depart without giving you any information and conversely, offering huge sums may not benefit you any more than a pittance.

Terrain Effects

Terrain (the geography of the land) played almost as much a part in medieval campaigns in this era as did the political considerations. The strongest castle, the distance to enemy borders and the defensive value of terrain were all weighed heavily by lordlings and their knights when planning a campaign. To reflect these considerations, certain movement and combat modifiers have been built into the game. Refer to the following table for these modifiers:

Type of Terrain	Effect on Movement	Effect on Battle Odds
Open Terrain	No movement penalty	No combat effects
Forest Squares	No movement penalty	Results minus 1
Mountain Squares	No movement allowed	No combat allowed
Swamp Squares	No movement penalty	Results minus 1
Castle Squares	No movement penalty	Results minus 3
Village Squares	No movement penalty	Results minus 1
Wizard with a Unit	No movement penalty	+1 Attack/-2 Defense
Lordling with a Unit	No movement penalty	+3 Attack/-1 Defense

Open terrain on the shire maps is represented by blank squares or squares with Roman Numerals in them. Roman Numerals represent peasant population. Forest squares are shown as green tree symbols. Swamps are represented by small white huts with green roofs. Castles are shown as red symbols. Mountains are shown as green and purple symbols. Coordinates at the top and side of each shire are to help players locate and move units or to cast spells. They are read, "A-3" or "H-10", etc. They have no other significance in the game.

COMBAT PHASE

Combat is caused when you move one of your flags into a square already occupied by an enemy flag. This can be as a result of movement made voluntarily or as a result of another battle in a different square causing unplanned movement. You may move *into* a hectare containing enemy troops but may move no further until the combat for that hectare is resolved. Combat is resolved by the computer by comparing the total strengths (knights and men-at-arms) of each unit, breaking that down to a simple odds comparison, "rolling the dice" and comparing that number to an internal Combat Resolution Table (CRT), then applying any modifiers, which results in the battle's outcome. All of this takes mere nanoseconds during which players can only watch as the outcomes are determined.

This is repeated for each battle (in order) caused by your movements. You must press [Space Bar] to move on from one battle to the next or to end the phase. This brief pause at the end of each fight gives players the chance to make notes, mark their maps or whatever is required before moving on to the next melee.

Combat in *Lordlings of Yore* is by necessity (and historical fact) quite bloody. In some battles entire units are destroyed and the victor left with one quarter, one-half or three-quarters of an attacking unit's original strength. In all cases, attackers will benefit from higher odds (more troops) and attacking in open terrain. Defenders will usually inflict some casualties on attackers even in very lopsided fights. The computerized dice roll reflects the uncertainty of hand-to-hand combat in this era. Attackers will never be able to anticipate exactly what may happen because of this random factor and the effect of any modifiers.

This method can produce some surprising results. The CRT has intentionally been kept internal so players will not spend so much time trying to analyze what *may* happen and simply deal with what *will* happen – much like commanders in the field did in medieval times.

Movement After Combat

Combat results will never leave two opposing units in the same hectare at the end of the combat phase. One unit will either be advanced, retreated or eliminated. Victorious units can be awarded as much as a two square advance while defeated units will only be retreated a maximum of one square. All retreats and advances are considered *Movement After Combat* and fall under the rules of this section which are controlled entirely by the computer. Once combat commences, several new battles (and any resulting advances or retreats) may occur – completely out of the control of any lordlings.

Retreats   Can be blocked by enemy units, enemy castles, maelstroms, mountains, dragons or the outer edges of the shire. If a unit cannot retreat during combat, it will *sometimes* stand and fight until it *can* retreat (especially if the unit has a lordling present) or it may "rout" completely, resulting in the unit's total destruction. On occasion, a retreated unit will fight to the death even if this requires several rounds of combat – particularly when attempting to storm a castle. Castle garrisons never fight at worse than five to one odds and are never forced to retreat, so plan your assaults carefully else your grand army may end up being not so grand.

Advances   Can be blocked by enemy castles, maelstroms, mountains, dragons or the outer edges of the shire. A victorious unit can be advanced straight into another battle if an enemy unit is in its path of advance. Advances *always* follow the original direction of attack. Retreating units always fall back (are pushed back) in the same direction the attacker used to attack from. Historically, defeated troops rarely ran any direction other than directly *away* from their attackers. *Example*: unit 1-A moves east to attack 2-B. Losing the fight, 2-B is forced to retreat and is moved one hectare to the east by the computer, thus giving up its square to 1-A.

Bribery

Bribery is accomplished during the [T]reasury Phase. Players may attempt to influence another player's movement or strategy by offering a bribe. Bribes are made in increments of 100 gold pieces and *can* total your entire treasury if you so desire but unlike other expenditures, you *cannot* exceed your actual treasury funds for a bribe. Gold is automatically transferred from your treasury to the treasury of the player you are attempting to bribe. There are no guarantees that performance will happen by the bribed player but that's part of the intrigue of the game.

Appeasement

Just like in real life, players may encounter unexpected events periodically that will affect their armies, their wizard, their peasants and even their ability to move units. These events can happen when you least expect them and may be positive events as well as negative ones. All players are subject to these events but in different ways and at different times. There is no way to anticipate them but no single event *should* ever be catastrophic enough to seal a player's fate.

You have the option during your [T]reasury phase to attempt to influence these special events in a positive way, should you choose to do so. You accomplish this by spending gold for [A]ppeasement which increases your **shire esteem**. Appeasement is always in increments of 1,000 gold pieces. The only limit to the amount you can spend for this item is the size of your treasury.

Broadly speaking, shire esteem is how well liked and respected you are as a lordling and ruler of your shire. The gold you spend for appeasement goes directly to the welfare of the shire and its peasants. The amount of influence that gold has on special events is in direct proportion to the amount players are willing to spend on appeasement. Players are never completely safe from special events when they pay for appeasement but the risk is considerably reduced by maintaining a higher shire esteem throughout the game.

OPTIONS PHASE

The sixth and final phase of a turn is the "Options" Phase. Players first receive word of any special events that may have occurred. These special events are directly influenced by the appeasement gold spent in the treasury phase. In addition, players have the opportunity in this phase to [C]hange their name or password if they so desire.

They can also send [M]essages of up to 80 characters to other players in the game. These are delivered at the beginning of a player's turn after a password is entered. Due to the vagaries of medieval couriers, there is always a chance a message may be intercepted by the wrong player, so be careful what you divulge.

Some veteran *Lordlings of Yore* players have even developed a simple code to use in messages. For example, 'H' might mean knights or 'X' might mean a lordling.

At this time, players can also generate a [P]rint of their shire map that shows terrain, troops, weather and dragons as well as all areas your units have mapped in other shires. NOTE: Printers must be installed in

Slot 1 and can be of any standard serial or parallel type. Some printers take several minutes to print a map, especially if there are a lot of units on the board, so be patient. *CAUTION*: If you try to print a map with no printer present, the game in progress may be lost.

As with other phases, players can review their [R]oster during this phase. When accessing the roster, press [Space Bar] to stop the listing and any key will return you to the menu or the map.

Players can [S]ave the game in progress at this time provided they have an [I]nitialized disk available for that. You can also [Q]uit the game if you wish. If you are the only human player left in the game, the game will end. If you quit and are resigning to another human (see "Swear Fealty" on page 32), that player will take over what is left of your army and assets. *NOTE*: See "How to Win" in the next section.

Hints of Play

How to Win

Winning in *Lordlings of Yore* ultimately is a combination of sound strategic planning, tactical expertise, wise use of gold and your necromancer and the ability to deal with a wide range of problems and options available within the game. Gaming experience will produce most of the battlefield expertise players need and you will eventually develop the ability to handle the myriad of options that may seem daunting at first. Much like chess, skill levels improve with time and effort.

Generally, this is not a fast game nor is it one you can master quickly. It is also a game some players find difficult to walk away from due to its complexity. The intensity level rises every time you are waiting to see what has happened since your last turn, this game being one of the few 48K strategy games that attempts to create the kind of "fog of war" that will keep you on the edge of your seat. That is especially true when fighting other humans as they are somewhat less predictable than the cp's.

Victory is accomplished when you are the only player left alive in the game or have achieved such overwhelming strength as to make it obvious to the other players that you cannot be beaten. It is not easy to determine the latter, as players cannot see all that is going on in the game that would make the above decision obvious. That is where messaging might be helpful - or taunting if you prefer.

You defeat another lordlings by either eliminating them outright on the battlefield or by destroying their castles. If you kill an opponent in battle, their treasury is transferred to your treasury and the remainder of their troops join your castle garrison for subsequent *redeployment*. In other words, they immediately disappear from the field and become part of your castle garrison, subject to the 99/999 rule.

An eliminated player's castle is automatically destroyed and removed from the shire at the end of the combat phase in which that player was defeated. All spells that player had active are also eliminated since their necromancer is now gone. A castle garrison that is attacked and eliminated destroys that castle's lordling as well, no matter where that lordling is on the map.

Should you eliminate a lordling in one battle and then be killed by their troops in that same combat phase (due to an uncontrolled advance or whatever) both of your treasuries and armies will be eliminated. Both castles will disappear as will all spells generated by both lordlings. If a player is slain in battle against a dragon, that player's troops and castle are eliminated and no one gets the remaining assets.

If you decide to [Q]uit the game for whatever reason and there are other humans still playing, you must SWEAR FEALTY (assign all your lands and property) to one of the remaining lordlings – including computer players. The conditions are exactly the same as in elimination except that in theory, the quitting player becomes a vassal (servant) of the lordling to whom they swore fealty. This actually was a far more common outcome of battles in medieval times than being killed outright. *NOTE*: Peasants in the home shire of a defeated lordling do *not* automatically become part of another player's assets. Someone still has to control them with their units in order to gain their taxation.

When you ultimately survive to become the last remaining lordling, you will be crowned *LORD OF THE REALM* and you will be shown a tally of your victory. This tally is in the form of a number which is your **victory score** for the game. This is determined by taking:

1. The gold left in your treasury.

2. The number of troops you had left in the game.

3. The number of dragons you have slain.

4. The number of castles and lordlings you killed or subjugated, then dividing that total by the number of days (turns) the game lasted.

In solitaire games, the number of cp's and their starting levels as well as the starting terrain are also taken into account. Victory scores are stored on the game disk along with your initials.

In addition to a list of victory scores the game retains, there is also a "verification code" that appears *one time* just before you enter your winner initials. This is the only time this appears and if you miss it, you won't be able to find it again. This code will be used for multiplayer tournaments to verify high scores, etc. Write it down, even if you're not in a tournament.

COMPUTER OPPONENTS

As many of you will find, it is difficult to get four people together in the same room to engage in a full scale game of *Lordlings of Yore*. We have provided for that by allowing the computer to play. It never gets tired, it never cheats, and it never taunts you – well, *almost* never.

At the start of the game, you will be asked how many humans are playing. Answer "1" for a solitaire game and the computer will command the other three shires. There will always be four players, regardless of how many humans are in the game.

You can also play two humans against two cp's, three humans against a single cp or four humans. The computer will react much the same way a human player does to a given tactical situation. You will not be able to bribe cp's. We tried. Imaginary gold has little value to a computer chip. You also cannot intimidate them with messages, etc. They can and *will* attempt to bribe, taunt or intimidate humans, especially on levels three and four.

New players should 'handicap' the game in their own favor when playing solitaire by setting the cp's on Level 1 and yourself on Level 4. Otherwise your gaming experience may be short and bloody.

STRATEGY

An old adage in warfare is, "The mental is to the physical as three is to one." This adage is quite appropriate when applied to *Lordlings of Yore*. The lordling with the most troops will not always be the strongest force in the game. Appearances can fool you, given that the fog of war hides more than you may think.

Players must maintain their composure and not panic when an enemy enters their shire. That may only be a feint by one opponent while another is poised to strike from a different direction. Yes, players gang up on other players. That's a fact, especially when facing three cp's on Level 3 or 4. In that situation, the cp's generally have only one objective - to wipe the human off the map.

Always keep a substantial reserve of troops in your castle except in the very early stages of the game when the enemy cannot possibly be close enough to attack. This both protects your castle and provides a strike force you can quickly deploy in your home shire if threatened. Above all, keep your lordling and necromancer well protected *at all times*. Winning in this game almost demands having both of those elements for any chance at success.

TOURNAMENT PLAY

This game is designed to provide each winner with a verifiable proof of victory. The reason for this is to make tournament play possible across a broad spectrum of the gaming industry. Players who returned their warranty card (included in the original 1983 package) with the game disk serial number on it, became eligible to enter tournaments as they were announced. Only one score per serial number was accepted, thus copied disks were not eligible. The verification system is still a great way to gain bragging rights with your fellow gamers.

Wizardly Hints

Trouble Booting Your Game Diskette

Troubleshooting a physical game disk is not likely to be a big issue, but here are a few things to consider. First, make sure your disk controller card is located in Slot 6 of your Apple II computer. Try the disk on a different computer or disk drive. Be sure your disk drive is stopped before attempting to remove the diskette.

Trouble Making Entries

Trouble making entries after the game has started could be due to the Caps Lock key being locked down. Check that first. If the game starts but won't respond to any keyboard entry, you may have a drive problem. Again, try the disk on another computer if possible.

Saving a Game

If you are having trouble saving a game to a storage diskette, and you are using an original *Lordlings of Yore* disk made in 1983, make certain that storage diskette was initialized *from the game program itself*. Normal DOS 3.3 initialization is not sufficient as the game must recognize a host of things to 'save' properly.

Printing

If you are trying to print game elements, your printer card must be in Slot 1. No other slot will work. Be sure the printer is ready to print when you press [RETURN] to begin printing or the game may lock up, causing you to reboot. You can get out of the print routine by pressing any key other than [RETURN]. Some printers can take several minutes to print from this game so be patient. Most printers should be compatible with *Lordlings of Yore*, but we cannot guarantee that.

Messages

Players sometimes become impatient with the messaging system –
especially when negotiating with Knaves. You can end viewing messages
by pressing any key. This is also true of the DEMO – any key will start
the game.

Passwords

If you are playing with friends and wish to dispense with the
inconvenience of passwords, simply use [RETURN] as your password.
This is also helpful when playing against computer players only.
Numbers also make excellent passwords.

[RETURN]

In this game, [RETURN] is powerful. Use it only when you are
certain of what you want to do next. Lose the habit of pressing it after
entries or you will pay a hefty price in lost turns, money or who knows
what. Above all, have fun with the game!

Conclusion

The designers have gone to great lengths to produce a highly playable and enjoyable game for players of all ages. Medieval warfare was, by its nature, confusing. Nobody had a cell phone or even a telegraph to send word of an enemy incursion. Movement to battle often took days or weeks. Weather caused delays. Peasants could be very testy. Villages were often hostile to their own lordlings. Once a battle ensued, casualties tended to be staggering.

Please remember this is a representation of a period of history most people know little about. We hope you will play it in that spirit. Your comments and suggestions are welcome, particularly in regard to the cp's as opponents. There are so many variables in this game, we could never hope to envision all that can happen. Your input may well help to improve an already terrific game concept. Above all, enjoy!

Notes For Programming Wizards

BY TREY C. JOHNSON

There are some programming techniques that I used in *Lordlings of Yore* that are somewhat non-standard for BASIC. They will not be directly convertible in other BASICs. However, there are always other ways of doing the same thing. I will try to describe exactly what those unusual routines are in this tech sheet.

Since I used Page 2 of the Apple II high-resolution graphics (location $4000-$5FFF) and free program space starts at $800, I was forced to use nine different programs all tied together to make *Lordlings of Yore*. Each program is approximately 14K (maximum) in length, and depending on your graphics memory allocation, it is possible that some of these programs could be combined to leave fewer files.

Throughout the game, I use shape tables, which is the Apple II version of a sprite. For example, if there are five shapes, the command DRAW 3 AT 50,40 would put shape #3 at location 50 (horizontal), 40 (vertical). I can select which group of shapes to use by changing the table pointer using POKE 232 and/or POKE 233.

Also, the command HCOLOR= sets the hi-res color to that number. (See the *Applesoft BASIC Programming Reference Manual* for the colors.) I also use no input commands to get keyboard data. Since I wanted to limit the input to certain characters, I used my own input routine. This was done in a subroutine, which could easily be made a standard INPUT command.

39

The Program Files

HELLO.BAS

This program loads in the initial necessary shapes, etc. and runs a demonstration of the game. The binary program call HELLO.OBJ which is loaded is basically four things:

- → The closed scroll (in a packed format)
- → The LORDLINGS script screen
- → The program to open and close the scroll
- → All the shapes used in the game

I also use a sequential text file, HISCORES, to store the top twenty high scores. When any key is hit, the program resets the memory and executes the program INTRO.GAME. INIT is a small machine-language program that I use later to initialize a blank disk for game storage. This program is not executed again until the game is reset.

INTRO.GAME

This program basically sets up the starting values of the game. The computer names are picked out of a random group of 28 names. The variables with a % (percent sign) after them designate integer variables. I used integer variables only to save memory. You may also retrieve a saved game from this program.

I used a simple technique to save the game in progress. I just saved all the variables to disk. When the game is loaded, everything is ready for the next turn. In this program (and all the rest) I use the series of commands VAL(MID$(STR$(SC%(L,X,Y)) ,3 ,1)) or something similar to get the value of a particular character of a variable. (i.e. if L=1, X=1, Y=1 and SC%(1,1,1) = 5678, the above example would return the value 7.)

There is one variable assigned to do nothing but determine whether or not a player is a non-human (computer player). It is KN(4). After all the maps are generated, the program falls through to PASSWORD PHASE.

PASSWORD PHASE

From this program on, in the first few lines a series of POKEs are made. These POKEs allow me to "cheat" when chaining from file to file. Since all my programs fit below Hi-res Page 2, and all my variables are above Page 2, I did not have to use a special chaining program. When I did, the variables were automatically shifted on top of the new program, or directly onto the hi-res screen. All I did was RUN the next program. The next program immediately resets the variable pointers to exactly where they were, still intact. This program also runs the COMPUTER PLAYER program if this player is not human. Otherwise, it falls through to the MAIN PROG.GAME program. PASSWORD PHASE is the first program at the beginning of every turn.

MAIN PROG.GAME

In the beginning of this program, all the variables for troops, weather, and dragons are combined into one variable for use later in the program. This was done to save a tremendous amount of space needed. This program controls going from one phase to the other. Most phases return back to MAIN PROG.GAME and then continue. DEPLOYMENT PHASE and MOVEMENT PHASE are both in this program.

NECROMANCER PHASE

This program is executed only if the Necromancer is alive and the player selected this phase. After you cast a spell, a little routine at the end causes a random message to appear. This was found to be very enjoyable to most of our playtesters. The rest of the program is fairly straightforward. It returns back to MAIN PROG.GAME.

TREASURY PHASE

There is nothing unusual in this portion of the program.

COMBAT PHASE

This program is fairly complicated. It uses a special Combat Results table designed by Jon F. Baxley to determine the outcome of a battle. During any combat, it was necessary to check if it was a castle battle, as that was handled differently. If you are killed (eliminated from the game) in this program, all your treasury, etc. is transferred to the victor.

OPTIONS PHASE

This incorporates several machine-language sections. The save-game (as mentioned above) merely saves all the variables to disk in three files (simple variable, array variables, and string variables). I also used my INIT file (by CALLing it) to initialize the blank disk for storage. By using the POKEs on line 185, I changed from my protected DOS to the standard one, and then back again. This program returns to PASSWORD PHASE for the next turn.

COMPUTER PLAYER

This program also uses tables to determine what the computer will do based on the conditions it finds in the game. The rest is fairly straight BASIC. This falls to either COMBAT PHASE or PASSWORD PHASE.

VICTORY SCORE

In the program, the score is converted to a code and the score, the player's initials, and the code is all saved to a file. The program then starts the disk over.

www.ingramcontent.com/pod-product-compliance
Lightning Source LLC
Chambersburg PA
CBHW021041180526
45163CB00005B/2235